EASY-TO-MAKE
CHRISTMAS
CRAFTS

Written by Judith Conaway
Illustrated by Renzo Barto

Troll Associates

Library of Congress Cataloging in Publication Data

Conaway, Judith, (date)
    Easy-to-make Christmas crafts.

        Summary: Directions for tree ornaments, cards,
and gifts to make at Christmas.
        1. Christmas decorations—Juvenile literature.
2. Handicraft—Juvenile literature. [1. Christmas
decorations. 2. Handicraft] I. Barto, Renzo, ill.
II. Title.
TT900.C4C65   1986   745.594'1   85-16475
ISBN 0-8167-0674-3 (lib. bdg.)
ISBN 0-8167-0675-1 (pbk.)

CONTENTS

It's Christmas time—and time for fun!
Here are some ideas for making your own
holiday decorations, presents, and some very
special treats. Have a good time making them
—and Merry Christmas!

SILVER BUTTERFLIES

These pretty ornaments are simple
to make. Why not hang a dozen from
your tree?

Scissors

Heavy-duty
aluminum foil

Pushpin

Paper clips

Ruler

Here's what you do:

1   Cut a rectangle out of aluminum foil
    for each butterfly. Each rectangle
    should be about 4 inches wide by
    6 inches long.
2   Fold the foil like an
    accordion. The folds should
    be as narrow as you can
    make them.

3   Carefully use a pushpin to punch a
    hole in the center of the folded foil.

4   Open a paper clip to look
    like this. Thread one end
    through the hole in the
    ornament.

5   Gently open the folds of the butterfly.
    Let it flutter from a tree branch.

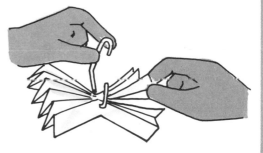

COILED FOIL ORNAMENTS

Here's what you need:

Aluminum pie plates

Paper clips

Scissors

Here's what you do:

1   Cut the rim from a
pie plate.

2   Starting at the outside edge of
the circle, cut the bottom of
the plate in a spiral, as shown
here. Leave a small circle in
the center.

3   Open a paper clip. Hook one
end around the center circle.
Hang the other end on your
tree.

7

CHRISTMAS SACHET ORNAMENTS

Hang these fragrant bundles, or sachets, on your tree—
and the whole room will smell like Christmas.

Here's what you need:

Red or green
crepe paper

Scissors

Bay leaves

Whole cloves

Stick cinnamon

Paper clips

Red or green yarn or ribbon

Ruler

For each ornament:

12- to 18-inch length of yarn or ribbon

½ Cinnamon stick

3 Cloves

1 Bay leaf

1 Paper clip

6-Inch square
of crepe paper

Here's what you do:

1 Cut a 6-inch square of crepe paper.

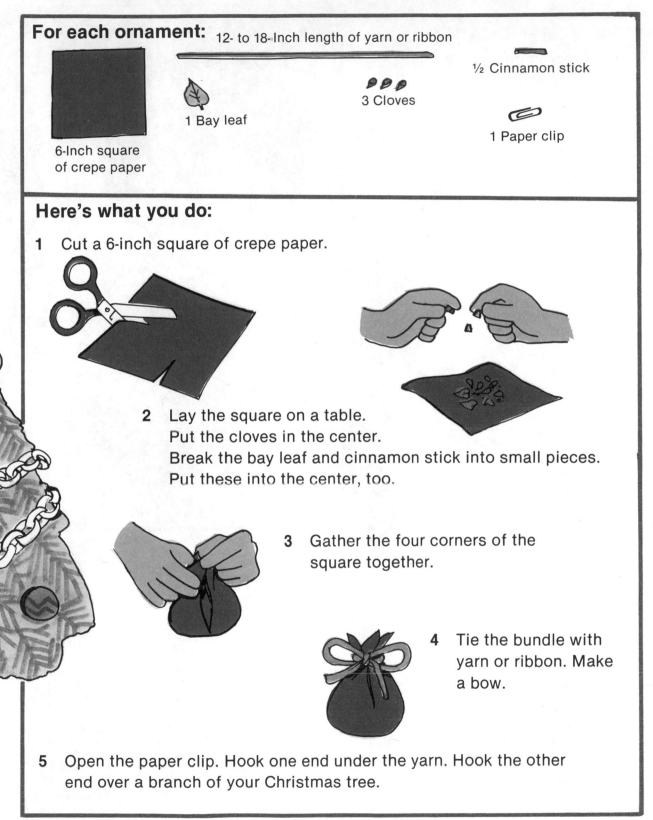

2 Lay the square on a table.
Put the cloves in the center.
Break the bay leaf and cinnamon stick into small pieces.
Put these into the center, too.

3 Gather the four corners of the square together.

4 Tie the bundle with yarn or ribbon. Make a bow.

5 Open the paper clip. Hook one end under the yarn. Hook the other end over a branch of your Christmas tree.

HOLLY-LEAF CHAIN

These colorful chains are fun to make. They look especially nice as decorations for doorways, windows, or along the mantel.

Here's what you need:

Scissors

Tape

Pencil

Green construction paper

Here's what you do:

1   Fold a sheet of paper in half. Cut along the fold. Fold each half in half...and then in half again. Unfold the paper. Cut the rectangles apart.

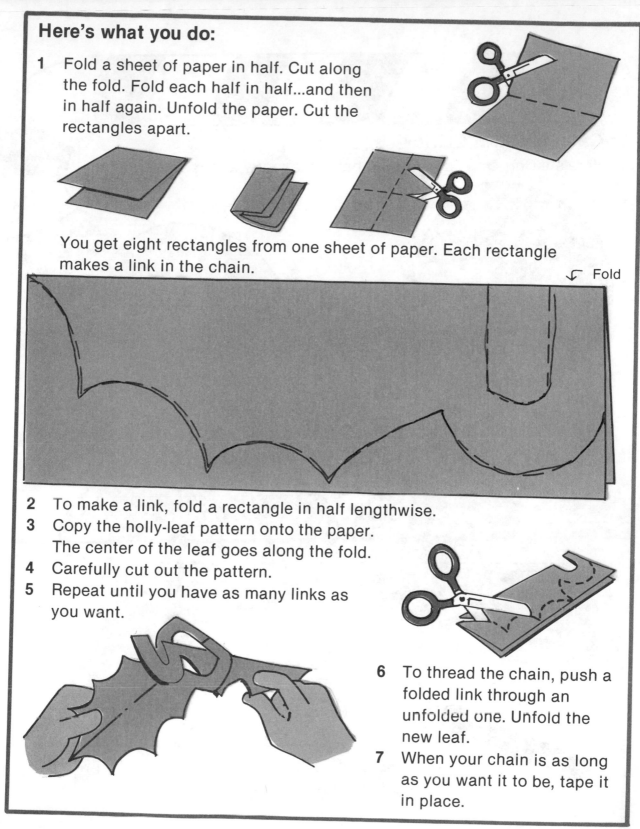

You get eight rectangles from one sheet of paper. Each rectangle makes a link in the chain.

↲ Fold

2   To make a link, fold a rectangle in half lengthwise.
3   Copy the holly-leaf pattern onto the paper. The center of the leaf goes along the fold.
4   Carefully cut out the pattern.
5   Repeat until you have as many links as you want.

6   To thread the chain, push a folded link through an unfolded one. Unfold the new leaf.
7   When your chain is as long as you want it to be, tape it in place.

11

CANDY-CANE CHAIN

Here's a Christmas decoration that looks pretty and tastes good, too.

Here's what you need:

Red licorice strings

Hooked candy canes

Ring-shaped candies

12

Here's what you do:

1   Fold a licorice string in half to make a loop. Place the loop under the hook of the candy cane, as shown. Bring the strings back up through the loop. Make licorice-loop knots on several candy canes.

2   To make a chain, tie the ends of the licorice strings together. Use double knots. Leave at least 2 inches of string on which to tie the round candies.

3   Put a ring-shaped candy on each end of the licorice strings. Tie each candy in place with a double knot.

ELF CHAIN

Santa's tiny helpers will dance merrily upon your tree.

Here's what you need:

Scissors

Construction paper

Pencil

Tape

Crayons

Here's what you do:

1 Divide a piece of paper into eight equal rectangles. To do this, fold the paper in half ... then in half again ... then again.

Unfold the paper and cut the rectangles apart. Each rectangle makes one link in the elf chain.

Fold
↵

2 Fold the rectangles in half. Copy the elf pattern onto each rectangle.

3 Carefully cut out the elves.
4 Use crayons to draw the elves' faces and clothing.

5 Hook the elves' arms together to make a chain. Then tape the arms together.

Tape

Tape

SANTA SAVINGS BANK

This bank can be used throughout the year to help you save money for Christmas presents.

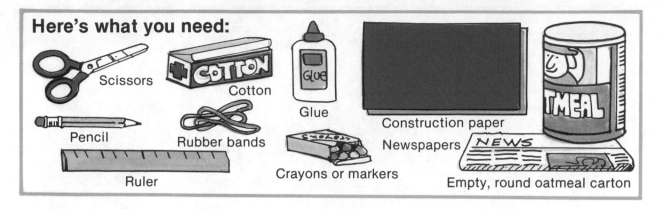

Here's what you need:

Scissors

Cotton

Glue

Construction paper

Newspapers

Empty, round oatmeal carton

Pencil

Rubber bands

Crayons or markers

Ruler

Here's what you do:

1 Place the empty carton on a piece of red construction paper. Using a ruler and pencil, mark off the height of the carton on the paper. Draw a straight line across the paper at this point.

2 Cut the paper along the line you have drawn. The large rectangle you have cut out will be Santa's clothes.

3 Place the red rectangle on some old newspapers and cover it with glue, especially on the edges and corners.

4 Place the carton on the edge of the paper. Roll the carton along until the paper is completely wrapped around it.

Use rubber bands to hold the paper in place until the glue dries. Wait until the glue is completely dry before adding Santa's face and hair. (Turn the page for more directions.)

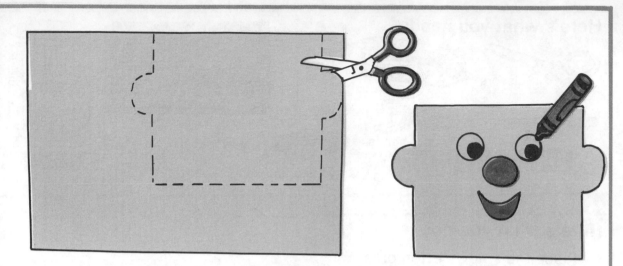

5 Cut Santa's face out of another piece of construction paper. Draw his eyes, nose, and mouth.

6 Glue Santa's face to the carton. Allow it to dry completely.

7 With your scissors, carefully cut a slot for coins in the top of the carton.

8 Following the shapes shown here, cut pieces of cotton for Santa's hair, eyebrows, mustache, and beard.

9 Apply glue to all pieces and put them in place.

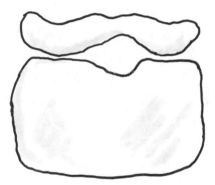

Here is how your finished bank will look.

SANTA'S HOUSE POP-UP CARD

These clever cards are sure to surprise your friends and family.

Happy New Year!

Here's what you need:

Scissors

Glue

Pencil

Crayons or markers

White construction paper

Here's what you do:

1 Fold a sheet of paper in half like this. Cut it into two equal rectangles.

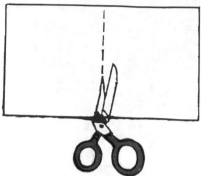

2 Fold one rectangle in half to make the card. The fold should be at the top of the card.

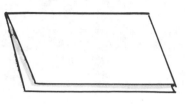

3 Write your Christmas message on the front of the card. Color it. Here's an idea you can use—or design one of your own!

(Turn the page for more directions.)

Tab

←Fold

Tab

4 Use the other rectangle of paper to make Santa's pop-up house. Fold the rectangle in half. Copy the pattern for the front of the house (shown on the opposite page) onto the paper.

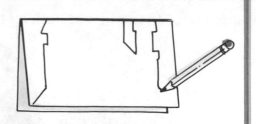

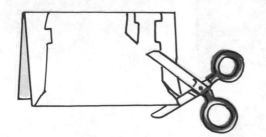

5 Cut out the house (cut through *both* sides of the folded paper).

6 Open the house and lay it flat. Color the house as shown. Do not color the tabs.

7 Glue the front and back of the house together. Allow to dry.

8 Open the card. Glue both tabs of the house along the fold. Write a message inside and sign the card.

9 Close the card. When the glue is completely dry, open the card to see Santa's house pop up.

CHRISTMAS BUTTONS

Make one of these bright holiday buttons for each of your friends.

Here's what you need:

Glass

Scissors

Corrugated cardboard

Colored paper

Tape

Crayons or markers

Glue

Pencil

Large safety pins

Here's what you do:

1 Choose a background color for each button. Draw circles on the pieces of paper by tracing around the rim of a glass. Cut the circles out.

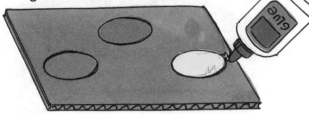

2 Glue each colored circle to the cardboard. Allow to dry.

3 Draw Christmas designs on each button. Use the ones shown here or create some of your own.

4 Cut out each button. Tape a safety pin to the back of each button.

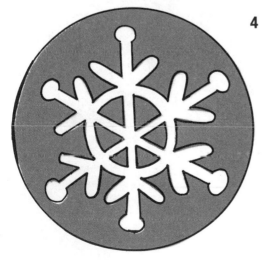

Wear the button with a smile!

CHRISTMAS CORSAGE

Here's what you need:

4-Inch square red paper

4-Inch square green paper

4-Inch square aluminum foil

Scissors

Glue

Tape

Safety pin

Here's what you do:

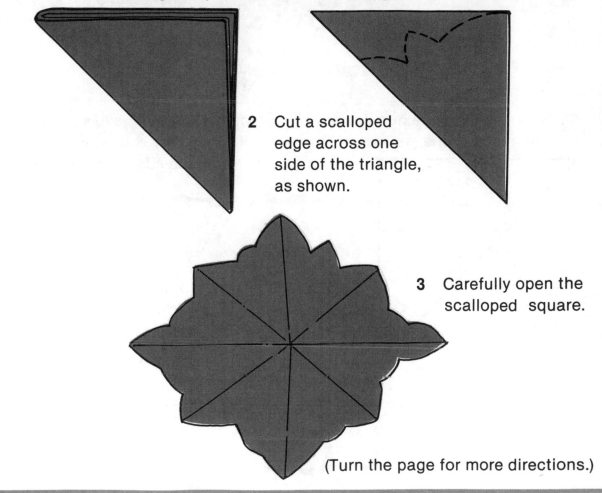

1 Starting with the red square, fold it in half, then in half again. Next fold it in half diagonally. You now have a triangle.

2 Cut a scalloped edge across one side of the triangle, as shown.

3 Carefully open the scalloped square.

(Turn the page for more directions.)

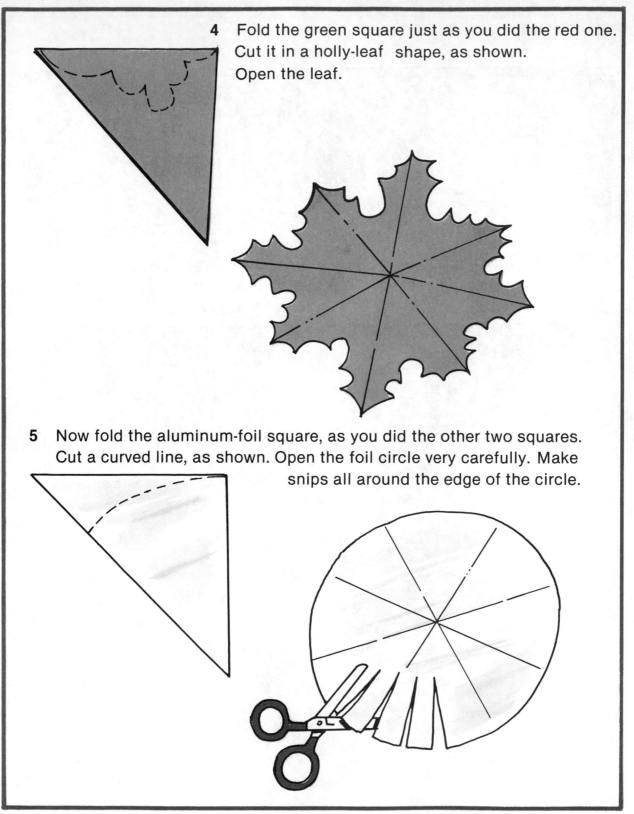

4 Fold the green square just as you did the red one.
Cut it in a holly-leaf shape, as shown.
Open the leaf.

5 Now fold the aluminum-foil square, as you did the other two squares.
Cut a curved line, as shown. Open the foil circle very carefully. Make
snips all around the edge of the circle.

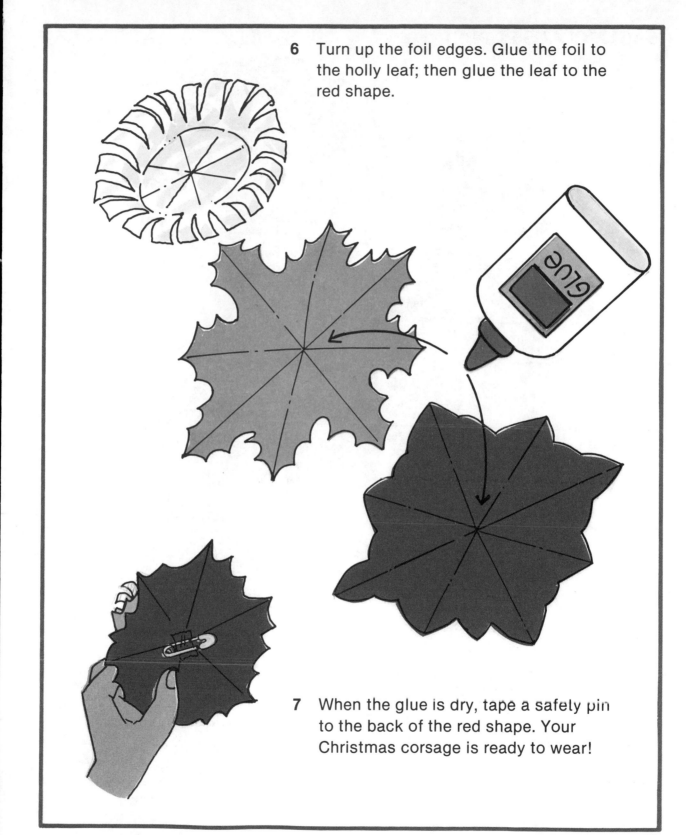

6 Turn up the foil edges. Glue the foil to the holly leaf; then glue the leaf to the red shape.

7 When the glue is dry, tape a safely pin to the back of the red shape. Your Christmas corsage is ready to wear!

SANTA CLAUS PUPPET

Here's what you need:

Crayons

Scissors

Cotton

Glue

Lunch bag

Construction paper

Here's what you do:

1 Draw Santa's face on the bag. Draw an open mouth, as shown. Part of the mouth is drawn under the flap.

2 Cut Santa's hat out of red construction paper. Glue it to the bag.

3 Use cotton for Santa's beard, eyebrows, and mustache. Glue them in place. Add a strip of cotton along the edge of the hat and a pom-pom for the top of it.

4 Place your hand inside the bag and open and close the flap to make Santa talk.

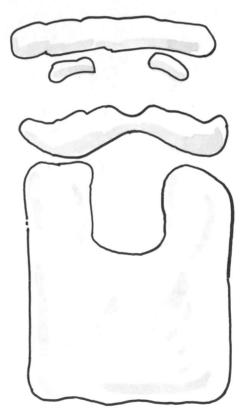

REINDEER PUPPET

You can create a reindeer puppet, too, with most of the same items used to make the Santa puppet on page 30.

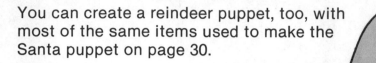

Here's what you do:

1 Fold a piece of red paper in half for the bow. Copy this pattern on the paper and cut it out. Open the bow and glue it in place.

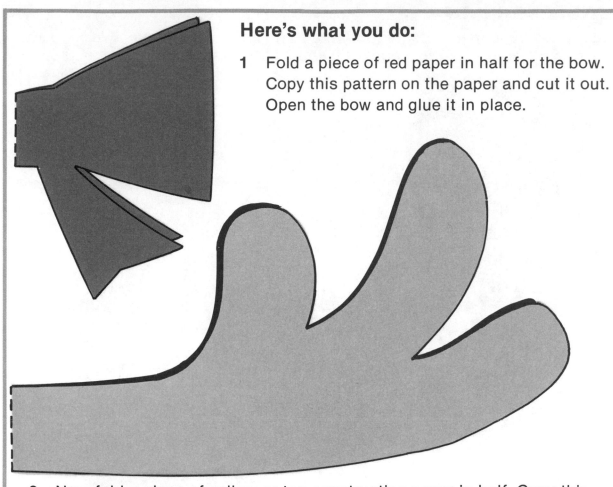

2 Now fold a piece of yellow or tan construction paper in half. Copy this pattern onto it and cut it out. These are the antlers. Open them up and glue them to the reindeer's head.

3 Cut out two ears from brown construction paper. Glue them beneath the antlers.

4 Using crayons, draw in the eyes, eyebrows, and nose. Add the mouth, drawing it partly under the flap of the bag.

REINDEER TREATS

Here's a delicious treat to leave for Santa's reindeer on Christmas Eve.
It's also a delicious treat for you! Eat it with milk and honey.

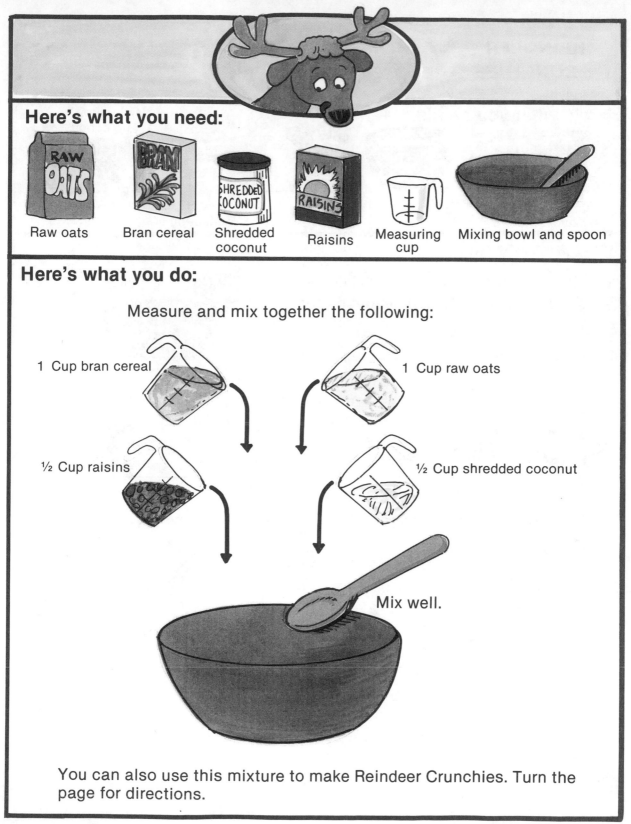

Here's what you need:

Raw oats · Bran cereal · Shredded coconut · Raisins · Measuring cup · Mixing bowl and spoon

Here's what you do:

Measure and mix together the following:

1 Cup bran cereal

1 Cup raw oats

½ Cup raisins

½ Cup shredded coconut

Mix well.

You can also use this mixture to make Reindeer Crunchies. Turn the page for directions.

REINDEER CRUNCHIES

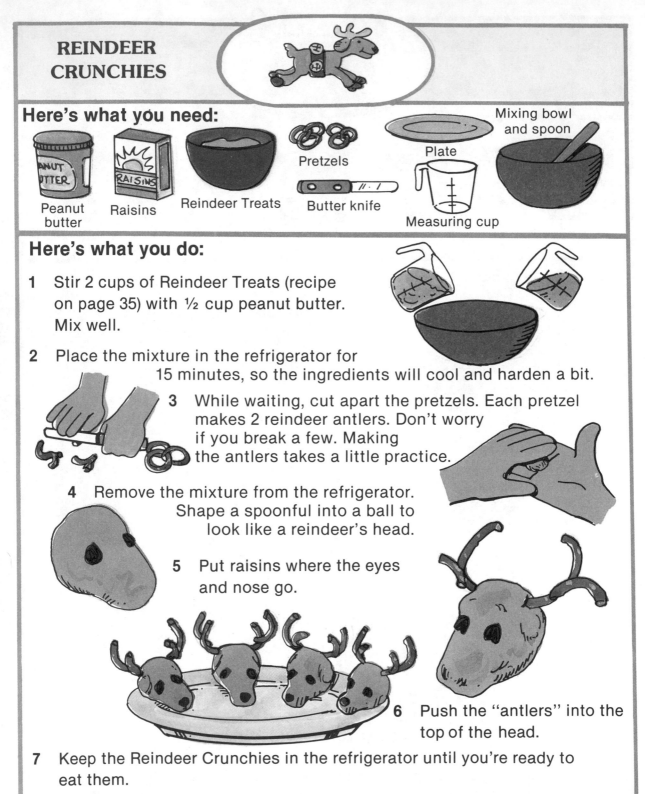

Here's what you need:

Peanut butter

Raisins

Reindeer Treats

Pretzels

Butter knife

Measuring cup

Plate

Mixing bowl and spoon

Here's what you do:

1 Stir 2 cups of Reindeer Treats (recipe on page 35) with ½ cup peanut butter. Mix well.

2 Place the mixture in the refrigerator for 15 minutes, so the ingredients will cool and harden a bit.

3 While waiting, cut apart the pretzels. Each pretzel makes 2 reindeer antlers. Don't worry if you break a few. Making the antlers takes a little practice.

4 Remove the mixture from the refrigerator. Shape a spoonful into a ball to look like a reindeer's head.

5 Put raisins where the eyes and nose go.

6 Push the "antlers" into the top of the head.

7 Keep the Reindeer Crunchies in the refrigerator until you're ready to eat them.

Here's an extra idea: Add a red candy nose to one of the reindeer!

CRUNCHY FRUIT COBBLER

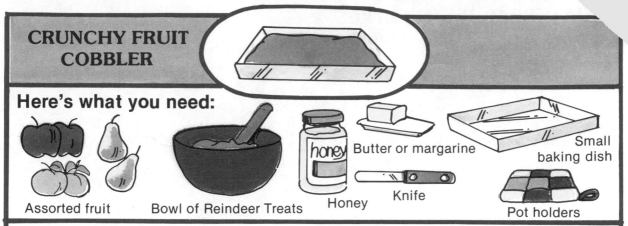

Here's what you need:

Assorted fruit

Bowl of Reindeer Treats

honey

Honey

Butter or margarine

Knife

Small baking dish

Pot holders

Here's what you do:

Note: If you are not allowed to use the oven by yourself, ask a grownup for help.

1 Set ½ stick of butter or margarine out to soften. Preheat the oven at 350°.

2 Slice the fruit, unpeeled, into small chunks.

3 Measure 2 cups of Reindeer Treats into the mixing bowl. Add the chopped fruit and 1 cup of honey. Stir until the honey coats the ingredients.

4 Use half of the softened butter to coat the inside of the baking dish. Cover the bottom and sides completely.

5 Pour the mixture into the baking dish. Cut the rest of the butter into small dabs and sprinkle them on top of the mixture.

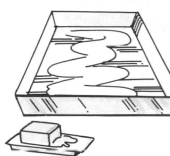

6 Bake for 20 to 25 minutes. Use pot holders to take the pan out of the oven. Serve the fruit cobbler warm, by itself or with milk or ice cream. Enjoy!

Here's what you need:

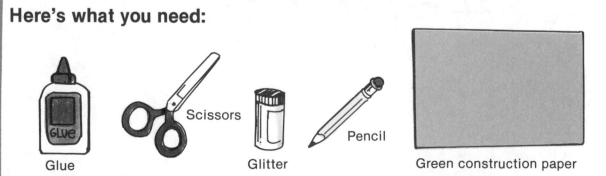

Glue

Scissors

Glitter

Pencil

Green construction paper

Here's what you do:

1 Fold a sheet of paper in half and cut it into two rectangles. (Each half makes one tree.)
2 Fold one of the halves in half ... then in half again ... and again.

3 Copy the Christmas-tree pattern, as shown. Carefully cut it out along the dotted lines.

4 Unfold the tree. Stand it up, so that the folds form a circle. Glue the two end flaps together. Now make the rest of the tree by gluing each section of the tree to the section next to it. Use lots of glue between the sections, letting it ooze out the edges.
5 Sprinkle glitter over the tree. The glitter will stick to the extra glue.

ELVES' HOUSE

Here's what you need:

Scissors

Crayons or markers

Glue

Pencil

Construction paper

This is the pattern for your elves' house. For further directions, turn the page.

Here's what you do:

1 Using pencil and construction paper, copy the pattern for the elves' house shown on page 41. Also copy the chimney pattern shown here.

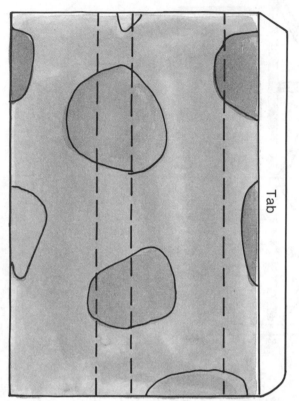

2 Use crayons or markers to draw in the doors, windows, roof, trees, and chimney. Color all areas.

3 Carefully cut out both shapes.

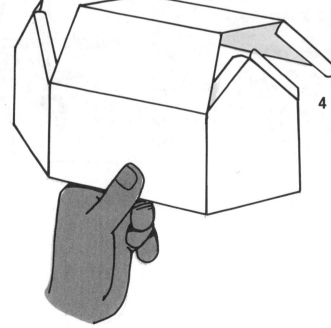

4 Fold the house along the dotted lines. Then apply glue to all the tabs. Hold in place until the glue dries.

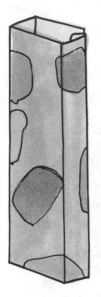

5 Fold the chimney as shown, and apply glue to the tab. Again, hold in place until dry.

6 Apply glue to the shaded area of the house. Press the chimney against it. Your elves' house is now complete!

CEREAL-BOX CHRISTMAS SCENE

Here's what you need:

Tape

Scissors

Glue

Cotton

Paints and brushes

Empty cereal box

Here's what you do:

1. Lay the empty cereal box on its side. Starting from the open end, cut an arched opening in the large side of the box. The dotted line shows where to cut.

2. Tape the slit back together, as shown. Glue the open end of the box closed.

3. Give the box a coat of white paint. (*Hint:* It is easier if you begin by painting the inside of the box first.) Let the paint dry. Then give the box another coat of paint.

4. When the paint is dry, paint the inside of the box sky blue. Paint Christmas designs on the outside of the box.

5. For snow, glue some cotton along the bottom of the box scene.

6. Make a miniature tree and an elves' house (see pages 38–43). Glue the tree and house to the inside of the box.

NOEL CUBE ORNAMENT

Here's what you need:

Sheet of white paper

Glue

Crayons

Scissors

Paper clip

Plastic tie

Pencil

Here's what you do:

1　Copy the pattern for the ornament onto a sheet of white paper.

2　Draw and color the designs on the cube pattern, as shown on the next page.

3　Cut out the ornament. Make a small slit in the star. Fold the ornament into a cube. Insert the plastic tie in the slit, as shown.

4　Glue all tabs in place. Allow to dry.

5　Unbend a paper clip. Hook one end to the plastic tie and hang the other end on a tree branch.

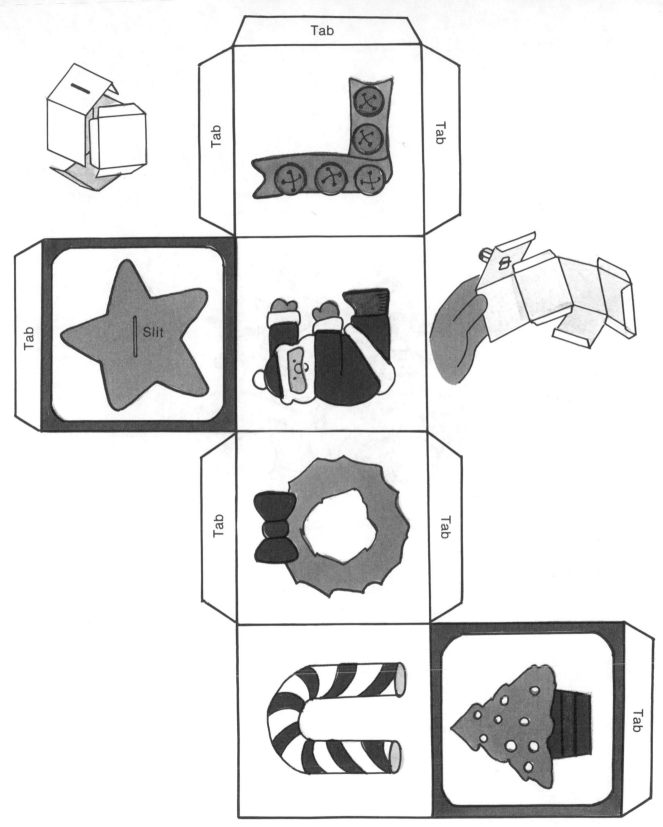